ALL THESE
THINGS AREN'T
REALLY LOST

ALL THESE THINGS AREN'T REALLY LOST

EGE DÜNDAR

THE **BLACK SPRING**
PRESS GROUP

First published in 2023
A Maida Vale Publishing book, The Black Spring Press Group
Maida Vale, London W9,
United Kingdom

Typeset with graphic design by Edwin Smet
Author photograph Can Dündar

The right of Ege Dündar to be identified as author of
this work has been asserted in accordance with section 77
of the Copyright, Designs and Patents Act 1988

*Editorial note: the author has generally used British spelling for his poetry.
The prose poems break randomly, as is the norm. Longer-lined poems have
been placed sideways for ease of reading. Every attempt has been made to
verify the correct spelling of all place names and person's names. We apologise
for any errors that may have managed to stay in, and ask you inform us for
later editions.*

ISBN 978-1-915406-34-7

BLACKSPRINGPRESSGROUP.COM

To mum and dad, in everlasting love

Portrait drawn in prison by Zehra Doğan, and gifted to the author
as a celebration of solidarity

Home, Tarçın and my mother [1]

"I try to hold on to what I remember, wondering where and what home is for me."

We grew up together. I vividly remember opening the door to see him on my father's shoulders, his confusion and his size, no larger than my mother's palms. Tarçın, mum called him, for his light brown fur: Cinnamon. His life had begun on a farm in Hungary, consoled by the warmth of his mother. One day, when he was only a baby, he was taken far away. As a child, I often thought about whether he would get a chance to reunite with his mother someday; whether he missed her, or if after all these years their separation was no more than a distant memory. I was a single child, and I felt he was the closest thing I had to a brother.

Waking up was always special. Before I had properly opened my eyes, I'd hear his clicking paws running up the spiral staircase, sliding slightly as he tried to turn into my room, bouncing onto the bed in a flash. His long ears and bulging eyes were the first thing I saw every morning. We'd play on the bed, as my eyes would come into focus. The sunlight shone through our seasoned window panes. I could hear starving seagulls yelling in flight; they were nesting in the crevices between our crimson roof tiles and lavender covered walls. My mother would then come in and push the windows open, the mimosas casting delicate shadows on the carpet. Sometimes she'd join in, cuddling. Sometimes she'd just stand there, looking at us, smiling, as if her piercing, arctic blue eyes saw through everything with ease.

It must have been about three years ago that he started falling ill. The last time I was with him – that is, the last time I've been home – he was as childish as ever, chasing kittens

1 This was first published in a fuller version in *PEN Transmissions*, 4th March 2019, English PEN's online magazine for international and translated literature. Many thanks to English PEN for permission for this to be exhibited here. For the full version, please see https://pentransmissions.com/2019/03/04/home-tarcin-and-my-mother/

away, barking incessantly at fallen leaves, scratching his paws on the parquet floor, impatient for walks. These were better days.

My mother called me late one evening. "The vet is saying he has this condition. The heart can't get enough oxygen." We could hear him wheezing through the night, gasping for breath. "Fluid builds up over time, enlarging it." Like anyone confronted with death I tried to hold onto his life. "Let me see him," I said.

She turned over her camera and there he lay, tense, breathing rapidly in his sleep as if he expected to be woken up at any moment. It pained me to be staring through a glass screen, no more than a voice echoing through his worried mind, unsure where the rest of us were. I wished I could explain what had happened since we had last met. How people were rounded up late at night, and how at sunrise it looked as though nothing had happened. How dad was imprisoned for his journalism, shot at, exiled to Germany.

How mum was illegally held hostage after they confiscated her passport. How the government had chewed up the aspirations of a generation and how I ended up stranded on this island, in London, having not seen them for three years. He was only seven years old. I didn't want him to think I had deserted him. At first, I was in denial: I knew I'd make it in time; I knew my father had used nothing but words, that he was neither a spy nor a traitor, that none of this should really be happening.

Tarçın's heart wore out. The last time I saw him on camera, he was panting in his cosy blue bed on the vet's table, tubes piercing his body. Every hour was consumed with stagnant updates. Our belief that he would make it slowly dwindled. Mum was beside him, holding whatever was left together. She didn't talk to us for two days after he died, as we mourned in each of our solitary lives.

I dreamt of him, a few nights after he died. He ran up to me on the front porch of our summer spot in Seferihisar. He was elated, joyous as I petted him. I noticed that there were bugs flying off of his skin, before he sped away like a stream of light across the yard, as if he had really missed running. I write his name on every fogged up window I find.

Perhaps it wouldn't have hurt as much as it did if people all across the country hadn't experienced similar upheavals. If my friends – model citizens: writers, teachers, students – hadn't been persecuted just like we were. If, still dignified, sometimes gravely ill, they hadn't been slandered and sent to jail for nothing. Waiting, incessantly, for nothing. If my grandfather, who I also haven't seen for three years, hadn't been diagnosed with Alzheimer's and I wasn't forced behind yet another glass screen trying to capture fragments of his fading memory. I try to hold on to what I remember, wondering where and what home is for me, without my return.

I reach for it in memories: the green tablecloth on our kitchen table; the sound of our doorbell; the rhythm of the sprinklers out front; the gatekeeper's whistle as he patrolled the streets; our ivy-covered garden surrounded by iron bars, sheltering us from the dimly lit street and the lurking gaze of strangers out there. Home lingers in my memories of conversations with Grandpa over Salep in winter, talking about his years as an imam in Bulgaria, pondering God and the universe; in my grandmother singing along to songs from her archaic kitchen radio, garlic from the frying pan, the feeling of her hands in my hair.

It lingers in my mother and me in the back of a beat up dark blue Peugeot, listening to Leonard Cohen: grumpy me, a 50 Cent and Eminem fan as a child, growing into a Cohen fan; our mission to find the hotel he stayed in after his Istanbul gig. Home lingers in the red bike my father taught me to ride, with the comfort of his hands behind the saddle, although he's long let it go.

I remember in pristine detail charging out the door and into the evening with Tarçın, racing each other and, foolishly, the setting sun. I remember the first time we ever saw snow with him, right there, in our garden. Where he now lies buried. All of these things aren't really lost. The past isn't just what has passed. It's a part of who we are. Maybe we are so eager for the future that we overlook the persistence of *then* in *now*. The past's permanence lies in our inability to hold onto it. Its transience makes it perpetual.

The state seized our assets. We were unable to pay our debts. Mum had to leave illegally, the home she built from scratch and her older family. Yet I've learned home is much more than objects or indeed a place. In my mind, her laughter accompanying the sound of my piano still echoes off the walls of the ancient cistern underneath our house. The one thing that hasn't lessened has been the only thing that stands against time: love.

My father and I, among many others, have been sent into exile for no good reason. I couldn't be with Tarçın when he died. Perhaps I won't see his grave or walk into that house again, but someday I will return to Turkey. Weary ferries will still oscillate between opposite shores, the afternoon light shattering into violet fragments over the Bosphorus. The streets and people I love will be older, some will have passed, but nothing will take Tarçın, my family or my country from me. I will remember how home grew under my skin. As I toughened up and as life, like a beetle, circled around a familiar street light, home shimmered with a warm hazel hue, guiding me through the dark.

CONTENTS

DOVE

On the outside of my kitchen window is an outline.
Traces of a dove, crashed, wings open wide.
No blood, simply the mark of its feathers and bones
meticulously printed on the glass,
as if it had just passed.

For days and weeks, rain and snow on end,
the figure stays there, untorn,
like the poor thing didn't just die but was also born.

It reminds me of a poem on empathy –
of the desire to be free,
and the result.
The unfulfilled wish,
to get through seamlessly.

Every morning I face it –
early in the kitchen having my tea or coffee,
the transience and permanence of life, gets to me
and the beautiful stains
of what remains, in between.

THE NIGHT AND THE LIGHT

Stains can't be seen in the dark
but are laid bare under the light.
Such is the disparity between
the night and the morning
black and white.

CELESTIAL WOMB

It's me
and these molecules I was brewed from.
Coagulated, an island, like the earth
encased in countless layers:
my mother and father,
but also the raw material
of our handmade table,
the roof we embrace under
and the dynasty of stars,
shining miniscule cracks,
through a titanic darkness.

The search was from where I started,
to where I've been all this time.
Loss upon loss I came to find,
what's once put together,
can't be fully torn aside.

Imagine!
The feeling of being up there, beyond the sky,
dazed in the sight of what we all feel,
whirling around.
Moving through the ages,
how folks once thought it stood on the backs of gods,
or the horns of a brazen bull, alas!

From such a distance,
you'd come to think eventually,
about just how the truth came so slowly,
but then, so suddenly and so clearly.
Space unveiled ahead; a quietude akin to death.
A blue cocoon behind, vacuumed

like the shelter that is a breath.
Steady gravity, an anchor
like our mothers, who ground us all.

We should remember and never forget,
how through the Dark Ages,
and Copper, Bronze, beyond,
in caves of mystery, we endured
and thrived and climbed,
and how the truth
came so slowly, but then
so suddenly and so clearly,
as we took off from the earth –
how it was instantly laid bare,
to the first sets of astronaut's eyes
that took a look back, over the shoulders of giants,
at what our borders and fables down below
would turn to seem.
The overview effect[2]
of knowing,
how all around us all,
everything was born and dear departed
in this celestial womb.

2 *Overview Effect – Space Exploration and Human Evolution,* Frank White
(Houghton-Mifflin, 1987) (AIAA, 1998)

STAINED GLASS

Headlamps flashing on your hurried steps,
and the frail posture of your left hand,
you hail a cab and I trace
your violet silhouette through the backseat window
down the street.
Stranded under the rain I turn onto South Bank,
a cigarette warm between my fingers,
and picture us near the Seine,
walking along the waking stream. Your reflections
clear and calm,
the purple kerosene of sunrise alight on your hair.
Standing against the glass walls of Mondrian hotel,
a season gently wanes,
parading as it sheds like the corroding gold of autumn,
lights, like diamond blossoms thread the streets.
I remember where we met in Chinatown,
in a shirt, a slim tie, rolled up sleeves,
my watch, grasping my galloping pulse,
minutes to midnight,
neon laced with candle light and paper lanterns,
us in the corner of a stairwell,
sheltered in our composed cosmos.
Talking for hours,
whispering into each other's minds,
telling tales ill-defined.
I catch a slant of your smile and the sleeping dark stream
sliding
down the side of your eye, accentuated, exposed.

Until on your fourth stained glass, you get up to leave
and time
leaks

through
the slow cracks
on the astral composition.
The light drizzle of the early hour falls on my shadow
and the pale paint of streetlights sliding
over damp pavements.
I walk in meandering lanes,
roaming, ever on
for home.

Photograph by Ege Dündar, Berlin, of his parents, Dilek and Can Dündar.

MEETING MUM AGAIN

Written to my mother on her first birthday in exile after three years of being separated from us.

was like listening
to the ceased wailings
of a man sick in bed,
or the yearnings of a dove, sated from solitude,
in the solace of the bevy's exodus,
ever grateful to the winds of years
blowing past scarecrows unknown.
Meeting mum again,
like the pages of olden notebooks
alight by kind candlelight, to remind and almost re-wind, time,
or sunlight suddenly reeling through the clouds,
paving a subtle path to believe in,
despite the bittersweet end to everything,
yourself
and thereby all else, on which you depend.
As a family on the mend,
meeting mum again
was like meeting love again.
Seeing through my eyes
or nearly hers,
capturing the cat's cradle of life
as it just unravelled,
around us.
My parents,
their fingertips reaching across time,
walls, barren fields and frantic despots
safely through each other's,
at an ordinary street crossing, like 'The Creation of Adam'
coupled as if they were never split,
when the sunset shot in,

like sunrise through the sky's sapphire skin, framed
between their arms.
Meeting mum again, meant she likely won't meet hers
again.
She had to make a heavy sacrifice,
leaving her home behind,
but in a twisted way –
that sacrifice was already made you see,
by the tides of time
and the frailty of memory.
It was her wisdom to understand it,
that set her free

to choose life over death,
one way or the other, forever,
as those who really survive, eventually do.

A SHOWER OF SUN

Love is a shower of sun,
there's no shelter from
and no shade to hide away
or be saved alone,
after its honest ways
have got you home.

As if one moment you are asleep in a waiting room
and it shakes you awake
to live closer to the edge –
tip-toe on its thin line,
hanging by a thread,
like when, through its flower shops
bakeries, hotels
and even nurseries,
the entire city, suddenly
carries her grace.

UNDER CONSTRUCTION

A labourer of words
sits,
scratching his numbered pages
with his finite ink,
carving,
in the alphabet of his feelings,
many immortal spirits.

BERLIN THROUGH THE CRACKS

"This is very much like Berlin" people keep saying,
as I hear stories of altruism in the city, "so typical of Berlin".
Mouthfuls of laughter, overflowing at every corner,
fights evaded before they started;
two people cussing and everyone and Haja, the Iraqi bar owner,
saying "Nein!"
breaking them apart like they did that worn out wall.
Both aggressors drunk, going for each other fast,
but held back, by a comfort zone of arms interlocked between them,
hate denied!
His fists go up, but in severe hesitation
almost to say,
"you don't really want me to punch you do you?"
"I don't really want to punch you, do I?"

We're just sitting at the table to the side of Till's local *spâti*,
chatting, learning, growing
and showing solidarity,
during the not so fruitful times of scaffolding
fencing the old shop,
for it provides and so do we,
for he's our age too,
Haja, who runs it, from Iraqi Kurdistan
and as Till says,
"he's a brother".

We're sitting on the sidelines
with German, Turkish and Sheikh friends
and later watching them
with an Irishman
reach out for each other.

He speaks Sheikh,
the Irishman,
even lived there
for a year
to enter a moustache competition.
He shits us not,
in Rojashar, Pushkar.
Caught in coincidence in a twist of accent and fate,
the Sheikh and Irish exchange some words
over which a connection gets made.

A mean beard on his face,
with a sailor hat,
the Irishman is figuratively an outsider to our table
he seems as if he's sailed the seven seas
and beyond,
to end up with a crazy dream
or something,
to take the world just as it was
no restraint on compassion
though to many it may seem obscene,
to trust each passing soul, whoever they have been.
"It's hard to understand for some," he knows.

They speak of Sheikhs and the Northern Irish
with the same churlish interest;
the sailor
tells us a story of being dazed,
in the world's biggest camel fair,
– someplace –
an Irish, Israeli and French Man
and that they couldn't get a single camel.
"They wouldn't tell us anything" he says
and I don't know if I really believe him
but it doesn't sound so far from the truth.

We drift off again,
along the night shifting past the pavement
talking now about
Dun Laoghaire in Dublin,
and my half-Turkish, half-Irish brother
– from another mother –
Cormac Coskun Barry,
who has been with me since the start
and will no doubt be till the very end.

I tell him, "Coşkun" means ecstatic in Turkish,
he gets it.
A homeless looking man passes by,
searching for a cigarette, saying
"Now you all be blessed"
when he gets it.
"Sorry to have to tell you that"
he carries on,
"but I'm a son of mother nature and identification is
wrong."
Tibet, Palestine, Lebanon,
Ireland, Turkey, India, Pakistan,
on and on you can go and the answer seems clear
partition is a bad example
of world-making,
that's why Berlin is great.
Berlin is amazing.

And the best part was,
how the Irishman first approached the Sheikh
saying,
" I mean you could be a piece of shit,
for all I know,
but every other Sheikh I've met was awesome!"
and we all knew about human rights,

and of the night too
and we all knew of love,
across the table
we had all felt it through.
And we all knew
that walls come apart
just as they go up,
and we all knew solidarity
and what it means to be free
without dreaming to be mighty.
How to stand by a guy just having a hard time
trying to get by.
Partition,
it's a bad example of world-making
and that's why Berlin is great.
Berlin is life,
through the cracks.

IN AN EMPTY PARK

The lonesome audience
of the silent afternoon;
swirling leaves on olden trees,
shelter my head and the pages on my knees,
ease my heart
with endless showers of applause
in the subtle breeze.

OVERCAST

The little girl ran across the park,
and I figured
when the sun shied away,
that it was getting dark.

But when she came running back,
through the gates
she had stormed out of,
the sunlight, too,
streamed back through the blue.

TO COMPASSIONATES

Written in gratitude to my fellow human rights defenders

Though the darkness may be lying in wait
under a glimpse of the setting sun, we will parade!
Not claiming this moment as evening nor day,
side by side, we will try to turn the tide
and stand tall, like empty glasses on a bar at close,
overflown till everyone's gone home
left drenched for the water of life, like those we stand up for.
Set to die for the possibility of prosperity
within the wretched run of the mill.

Though we may not counter the darkness
stretching in tall shadows
amidst dim lit streets,
from where our fellowship meets
there shall ever be reinforcements.
Torches alight as warning and shelter
in sight, however near or far.
Thanks to your wishes on falling stars,
by the time a hasty darkness crawls
sweeping through the cities
trailing close,
our search for the destined dawn
will have long begun.

LI DU MAN (WHAT IS LEFT BEHIND?)

Written on 7th of May 2019 at the Li Du Man (What Is Left Behind) exhibition at Tate Exchange [3]- curated by Ege Dündar, in collaboration with Nusaybin which was razed to the ground by inhumane military operations.

I asked,
What is being carried to this gallery?
when I first walked up to this floor,
in two suitcases Zehra carried by her petite, firebrand frame.
Is it what remains or what's lost? Objects or fragments of home?
What was the scent that permeated through our breathing?
Was it discomforting?
Was it slaughter or war?
Displacement or death of another sort?
Could these carpets, scatters, drapes and
bloodied woollies for babies
be revived? Can we look through the burn holes,
and what would we see?
Are these victims of impossible causes or military
impunity?
Are they what survived the ruins?
And is it the parts that stuck on, ruptured nonetheless
that makes us remember,
or the parts ripped off and burnt
like flesh and bone?

Do they not embody, as they are, what they once were?
Or is that for us to make out and give life to by care?
Are these fallen artefacts
half the people that once owned them?
Are they alive if "they" are slain?
Are they so distinctly theirs
they could never come to hold the same sense of home
for you?

3 https://counterpointsarts.org.uk/wp-content/uploads/2019/12/2finallidumansmall-1.pdf

Maybe you're here by chance,
can this not just be your home, too?
And the tattered textiles on our scorched, communal carpet
all made of our own colours and shapes in unison,
over the earth?
That's what Zehra thinks anyway.
But you,
you have a very particular way of looking at the world.
So see how you feel,
make up your own mind.
As these scarred artefacts of home swerve all around me
from Nusaybin, Turkey
to the Tate Modern gallery,
towering over the river,
leading out to the boundless sea.
I see faces, young and old
sprung from London and all abroad,
inspired to listen, tell and bridge the gaps
I've come to believe that they are indeed still alive.
Like Zehra, still they are an integral part,
in the palette of where they once were.
Home is never truly lost,
so long as fragments or
a soul endures,
and lives to tell others.

THE BAZAAR IN GELSENKIRCHEN

Hüda means 'God' in Turkish, *Verdi* means 'given'. This was
the assumed fate of my friend who was born here, not by his
choosing, but who has lived here, clawing through each day
with his chopped nails and his untarnished spirit. I'm not sure
of the day, as I expect he couldn't pin it down either when he
made up the escape for his mind.

"It moulded, you see," he tells me,
as we're speeding like a fearless bullet 200km/h+ in a
Volkswagen down the autobahn,
"over time."

*

The lack of a challenge is often why people choose small towns
in maps stretching wide as the sky, in a "globalised" world.
It's comfort. It's the sweet sense of time slowing down, the
undemanding mundane taking hold. The security in knowing a
cultural code so well, that you no longer think about or beyond
it, to the point that any surprise is a stranger
– that could also signal danger –
Happiness lies anchored on the backs of others, so much else
over the backs of everyone else seems stale.

*

As we pull into the petrol station beside the Burger King
reeking of that tasty fried oil and petrol,
"Here," Hüda says, "is where work for me began."
I take my sunglasses off as I get out of the car following Hüda's
lead. A few trucks, as long as bridges, rest as if for a deep
breath in the back alley. Hardened, light blue strollers for car

polish greet weary travellers, like great Roman columns at the gates. Tubes line the walls under fluorescent lights shining on dampened walls, a dark green hue breaking through pale white tiles. Filth, encased in soap draining through the cesspool.
A Spaniard owns the car wash, his green tilted sports car seated in the middle of the runway – under intensive care – lays the rest of the carwash bare, and no one dares or even can stare too long for fear of jealousy, the kind their evil eye amulets fall short to shelter from.
The workers wait by its side as if by the cradles of their babies, trying hard to keep them asleep.
This is where Hüda first worked and wondered why it was that his *Usta* was a heretic in the eyes of his brothers at the local mosque, despite the fact that day in, day out, he helped everyone he saw – with all he had – despite the fact that he was one of the nicest people Hüda and the neighbourhood had ever known. That he somehow felt, even as a kid, that there was no place for evil in this man's heart, none at all.
"Why?" Hüda wondered,
"Was he a sinner who would eventually go to burn in hell?" Despite the fact that he had the tightest work ethic, for 1,100 Euros a month, opening his carwash at 6.a.m sharp, each morning and often staying for urgent customers into late nights.
He used to run around fixing their wheels before turning to tend his own. Theirs turning much faster perhaps, or a larger cycle – we also spoke about this with Hüda – about how to break the fact that, the wheel only gets bigger to thread as you get better in what you do. Eventually, Hüda wondered, did his *Usta* not deserve a glass of beer,
or a piece of heaven, after being so good all over?
And why was his drinking such a sin that overshadows pretty much everything he had to give within to his brothers at the mosque and the neighbourhood folk whenever he saw them? Hüda saw his brothers at the mosque in brothels and dirty

money deals, repeatedly, knowing well they would go home to their wives and amidst the people they conned.

Hüda wondered, as he looked upon them. Itching to trick but failing to treat, he wondered as they chose, strictly what he is to eat and to be, what not to eat and not to be as they mend to bend the rules in favour of their favourites, and frown upon questions that question the ways in which they act as they hesitate to question themselves instead.

Swimming in their spiteful whispers, Hüda says he almost drowned and his *Usta* was a life-vest and that's just the way he seems and feels, as he offers us orange juice in plastic cups alongside pastries from Turkey, as he embraces us at his ramshackle door, as he embraces his monstrous bulldog: Pasha.

Pointing a water gun at him when he misbehaves, despite being almost more than his size. Pasha understands.

*

"Hüda is like my third son" *Usta*'s wife says, caressing the sun-lit side of his face and Hüda replies:
"And you are like a mother to me, like Merkel by the way!"
Usta and his humble bunch now start to grumble over the problems of the German government.

Usta thinks Chancellor Merkel was mistaken to let those Bulgarians in, that they cause havoc. Fooling, raping and stealing from the innocent. Hüda seems surprised as he kindly reminds his *Usta*:
"That was exactly what they said about us remember? '*Scheisse* Türken'?"
Besides it was not Merkel's decision but the EU's "rushing to promises proven false...Welcoming Afghans, I mean, the Syrians," he adds.
"All the same..." *Usta* shrugs.

*

In the process of belonging, you forget "others" so easily.
As you climb the steps in society, looking down can get
harder. It pains me to see how these were the same slurs
damned upon *Usta*'s kinsmen, the Turks and the Kurds,
once upon a time and still – while neither yet lives in those
houses on that promised hill. As I said, *Usta* doesn't really
say much, but his actions you can read like a book. The
clarity in his mentality shows how he couldn't hurt a fly if
he tried.
His wife tends a garden in the back yard, raising most
anything she used to eat back home, and cooking it for
her family. There is space for a big blow-up pool for her
kids and a smaller pool for Pasha; you can feel her infinite
grace in a single touch of the hand. Her resistant humour;
an armour's shine on her laughter. Her hospitality shows
not only in the way she dresses the table in a snap with
whatever they've got left, but also it shows in the scars
on her sprained ankle, trying to help a neighbour start his
motor, in how she gives up her corner seat and takes the
plastic chair in her own home, which she clearly views as
all our own. Even over a few hours, I too, feel as though I'm
one of her children.

*

By the time we get there, the Bazaar is a boiling pot full to
the brim, resting in the car park of FC Shalke 04 Stadium.
Every weekend, the Bulgarians alongside the Polish,
Syrians and the Turkish and Kurdish sell life, or whatever
is left over from theirs. Short tents intermingled, almost
melting from the heat.
Underneath, hustlers selling broken clocks, plastic hearts
and all sorts of things in the summer heats' high. There's

mainly fake jewellery and thick lingerie, old electronics,
golden rings and watches, rugs and bunches of living room
lights.
A beheaded mannequin's legs rest dressed up in lingerie.
The head resting on tracksuit pants and cheap price tags.
Like some twisted monument, with its back to the various
kinds of diamond shaped, plastic chandeliers sold at the
neighbouring stand.
This is a place where rough and ragged men sell children's
toys, steel workers sell mixed CDs, children sell
second-hand,
half-naked
or half-bodied Barbies, that go for even cheaper –
wedding dresses and Burkas packaged side by side, and
bras unlaced lined out back.
The toys made up of police cars, dancing ducks and bright
dogs wearing sunglasses, sold by a truck driver scratching
his beard and pants.

*

This is where
scarred kids beg in silence and the city folk dwell and
frown on the prices, on the quality and the people too,
though they'd hate to admit that –
This is where Turks diss the Bulgarians diss the Polish,
diss the Syrians engulfed in each other's conditions,
in the bazaar in Gelsenkirchen.
This is where Hüda was born and grown and made it
through such often-neglected walls
as he insists,
so long as imperfect folk like his *Usta* and himself persist,
seeking not what is pristine but what's plausible,
that everyone else can, too.

GHOSTS IN THE WIND

There are ghosts in the wind,
crawling over the skin,
I can feel them within but
to my eyes they won't give in.

They take flight when I depart,
trail till I arrive, like an alibi
or a reason to leave things behind.
All the restless movement a telling sign,
that we're all haunted, in the mind
by our ghosts in the wind.
Concealed like a sin,
roaming over the borders of what has been,
for everything that never arrived,
there are ghosts in the wind, they'll live until I die.

These ghosts, they never lie
hanging beside every station
and behind each destination,
right after each goodbye
stressing, we could go further if we tried.

Ghosts in the wind,
– like a senseless longing –
won't let that restless feeling die.
Ghosts in the wind, a telling sign,
that what we are not,
– like our shadows –
we also carry by our side.

AT 7.03

I sat down thinking about
the way a tree incarnates the day's last light
with its leaves,
like kindling upborn against the dark,
igniting for a shivering moment
the echoes of a violet glow,
parading against shades and shadows,
as late as the eye can see.

7.03
spelled the time when
I turned around to meet you,
in a run-of-the-mill pub,
the darkness in free-fall,
easing into its expanding exoskeleton,
pulling the ropes of our entangled minds
through each other's
and slowly up at the moon.

At 7.03
in the projection of my eyes
are the colours of another,
dipped in for a moment before passing by,
without being much mindful of itself,
or of all the rest.

At 7.03, when we were encased
by an illusion of elation,
I pressed on and walked through the colour,
down the pit of the well,
and embraced the absence of light at its core,
colour was but a diving bell.

I felt like a newborn,
complimentary swerve
to counterpart her balance
and imbalance,
a leaf, unravelling within its cradle of skin.

At 7.03,
the pre-historic glow of colour
radiated through
her eyes and dilated my blood.
The machinery of my body,
suddenly derailed from orbiting its centrepiece
by the magnetic glitch,
of the colour I can't remember or forget.
It holds a key.

At 7.03,
we knew not to know what to see in each other
and when I turned around,
the voices harmoniously chiming
through the echo chambers of lungs and glasses
had shattered, hanging soundless, meaningless,
mid-air,
and there was no telling if that was you
or if you were even aware.

ROOTS OR BRANCHES?

The underground or above?
Wasted or nurtured?
Envy or love?
Homeless or forlorn in a home?
Day or night?
See or be seen? Devise or dream?
Can be all or in between but cannot be the one.

Knotted trying to command,
a circus of confluences you reprimand;
vestibules that lure you in
to learn, to change, to love...
For they were never long enough,
unchained anchors have long been left to rust.
Set sail on what remains,
like pine, larch and oak
what you keep, will keep you afloat.

A window must've been left open,
but a curtain nailed unspoken
has cloaked a taste for light.
Come take a peak,
each composition can shelter all that was once set alight.
Who we once were, is here with us tonight
as frantic fractals in shadows
dancing out of sight,
leaving as they torch trails,
a charcoal moonlight,
somethings must remain –

As the future turned looking for the past,
home, it grew under my skin,

as I got roughed up, as life circled
like a beetle, beating around a familiar street's corner light,
home; it lit up,
a lonesome hazel hue, guiding the path
into the unknown.

Now these deafened spirits dwell,
through the ages and the pages of history that will pass,
dusted and set free at last
when forgotten,
like all we now remember.

LUNAR MARE

I hear your little heart hurling in its tight chest
wheeling another cycle of breath as we sit in a ramshackle theatre,
devoid of our voices, in the dungeon of the dark
two seats apart.
I sense your presence like a lunar mare,
even your figure barely there.
Voices up on the stage address us, forsaken lovers in the crowd,
"To live with fear is a life half lived!"
"Fall in love!" the actress cries
"during senseless tragedy, whisper 'this is good for me.' "

We watch in awe,
as all this charade silently slips through our ears and tightly zipped lips
settling just under the tongue.

The lights come on, and frenzied to hide feelings like a blush, people get up,
walking out of the theatre behind tightly fastened intricate masks.
Sunk in my seat
I recall us laughing on the naked grass,
cloaked by our clothes soaked in autumn's colours, interlaced in the rain.
Me tapering thin, shedding pages like skin,
down to earth, without ceremony,
as if to repent for sins.

Grief lurks by the bar as we leave the scene,
we are unsure about making it through,
climbing down the velvet dressed steps overlooking the busy avenue,
where love once streamed down every street,
came whistling, out of the blue,
when the night dissolved in hues.

Now sheltered, but in a home forlorn; we lead each other on,
rooted as much as boxed in,
by the afterglow of what has been.

WITH A BLANKET (2011)

The room is dark,
no shadows.
"I can't see" she says,
I switch on the light.
Her face, a glass of wine
spilled on a white carpet.

The bulb burns out.
"I am thirsty" she says,
the kitchen is cold
the fridge, broken.
"How do you live here?"
her voice,
a rusty kitchen chair.
I answer
"With a blanket".

A cold night, autumn, a cold bed, winter
a calendar, a year.

"It's late," she says,
looking out the window, "just let go."
She walks out,
I look at the clock,
it stops.

I grab a blanket.

RAINY CLOSET

To get a pass from our restless past,
you lift all the weight,
and stack it onto my overhead closet.
But no one's there to stare at the ceiling
and the room is bare, so it all saturates.
Still and cold, hanging in the air like rain to fall
or some tale of old,
with no one to carry it
but our memories,
like clear skies fading.

Wasn't this just what Lennon meant when he said
memories lose their meaning,
when you think of love as something new,
and we sang along then.
The echoes of our croons, a voice as one,
shattered and grew like moss
along the lonesome coast.
Our love was neither young nor old
when it found us and took hold,
like a ship stranded between two ports
dreamt as life and death,
and I would sigh on its sails days on end...

You lift the longing, the guilt,
and the traps of time away
in large stacks onto my overhead closet,
which is now abandoned free
from you or me,
hanging in the air
like a raincloud,
often pouring
from cracks I seldom see.

A TRIBUTE TO GEORGE COWLING (2010)

I turned on the light and filled water in the bathtub.
Removed my watch,
pushed my hair to the back like George Cowling[4],
not a minute
particle of hair out of place, and watched the water trapped in the tub like colours in a drawing
or smoke in a cigarette.

Cigarettes.
I just felt like one laying down in the bathtub,
that first sensational rush of nicotine through your blood like drawing
a watch
with no minute
hand or watching George Cowling

4 Britain's first BBC TV weatherman.

talk in your living room for the first time. I love George Cowling,
the way he tells me its gonna rain in London as often as I smoke cigarettes.
It must have been 1954 when I met him. When toys and conversations were replaced by 10 minute
shows in a box Dad brought home with bathed breath. Unruffled, I splash the water in the bath tub
with my left hand and watch
the water drawing

driblets on my face. I wonder if a drawing
could be colourless, transparent or just black and white like George Cowling,
as he watches
me smoke a cigarette,
sitting in the bathtub
and waiting for the news, a 10-minute

snapshot of life. Minutes
pass like drawing
cards out of a tarot deck, trapped in an apartment like water in a bathtub,
I dream of meeting George Cowling.
Wondering what I'd say. Maybe offering him a matey cigarette
or tell him how much I adore his watch.

I watch
other presenters too but no one else can talk about clouds for minutes
and still smile like one does smoking a cigarette
after sex, or winning the Christmas draw.
It starts to rain outside and George Cowling
grins in victory as I step out of the bathtub.

I check my watch and take out an occasional cigarette;
through the bathtub, water is set free minutely,
as I draw the curtains, and wish good night to George Cowling.

YEARNING

I hear it coming like an early train above,
wheels glazing through cold steel,
the sun uncertain of its wake.
I look out of the manhole from the sewer,
the mass sprawl of streets are patched-up
with a laboured bleeding,
quiet as a creek,
percolating into the loop hole.
Passengers adrift through the city's vessels
under the skin
where many of the blinded, the likes of myself,
live in ghostly premonitions of online presence.
It's the 21st century and walls are built with screens.

Labyrinths thread, in and out of sight,
carved with screeching anvil railways lines,
carrying urbanites, yearning for cabins in the woods,
for the fresh wind's subtle tease,
blowing interlaced
with the weight of their breaths, swimming
on a nacreous moon over a darkened lake's sunken chest.

Underground, sheltered from the streets,
where dogs sleep on iced pavements,
people dance, dazzled in sound
and a coruscating kaleidoscope of neon,
nerves zapped like flies on electric nets.

I look out of the manhole,
my skin bleak as bed sheets,
and stare shrivelled at the grand texture
of bleached clouds

curdled, sweeping the sky,
the moon,
like a bedside gaslight,
faintly by the morning arriving.

Day breaks through as the night gives in,
workers and dancers change shifts
leaving us all on a thin line;
one step between leaving to defy
the disguise leaking into the machinery of our minds,
– or staying to watch it swerve deeper into the nerve.

Everyone is yearning, so I search my notebook
for what I found where we met,
two stranded figures shuffled out of deck
and freeze on ceremony for the memory –
before the train pulls away,
cutting across that estranged, downtown jive
and I climb down to the dampened sewers,
nurturing echoes of its sharp wheels departed.

THROUGH THE MIRROR (LYRICS)

Well, I feel I'm on the edge of my senses,
prowled and scared, the fear, evermore real
in my own, old, beckoning mind
a longing I hide
speaks when I rhyme,
where the sea meets a sky undermined,
a path leads onto my ways,
I'm owed to the road on which I stray.

Coming home to my lone remains
half of everything suddenly missing,
me, you, forlorn in the blue,
till you look through the mirror and you see me inside.
When you look through the mirror and you see me inside.

Now you ask me, why do I try,
to break this ancient divide,
'cause the stars did collide,
to set our lives alight,
to untie a tongue, that I know I speak,
well I'm here and you are
till the light comes to die
and truth will arrive, if we wait by its side.
Now the night, will proceed
from my view and the blue,
will grow to conceal
the flame in the mind,
well I'm here and you are
and we're bright as the sun
and truth will arrive if we wait by its side.

So come meet me there,
come meet me there,
where the mountains grow in snow
where a mist springs anew,
and behind a shroud of vines, defiant our mind
lingers in reveries.

ELEVATOR ENCOUNTER

Their story begins
when the man's car approaches the tall building,
a slide through the red light, perfect timing,
and the woman walks out of the shop,
both, unconsciously racing, to catch a future moment when it happens,
the man opens the door for the woman to walk through,
she having left 20 minutes ago perhaps
and him an hour or so.

In the lift,
– like the legend of Orpheus –
they can't contain themselves from a look,
and catch each other on a quick glance through the mirror
before their eyes hurry back down to the feet
after being momentarily exiled into one another's.

Two mirrors on each side, cast a perpetual range of reflections
there's a restlessness in the avoidance they both keep,
until the doors slide wide open, steps echoing down the hallway
breaking the custody of silence.

Yet in their minds, the moment lingers like fog on glass
rapidly vanishing,
and what it meant, that they both said nothing.

AUGUSTE RODİN (1840-1917)

A poem from the titles of sculptor Auguste Rodin's artwork
(written in his museum in Paris, 2010)

Alexis Rouaier
watched modern Paris
from *The Tower of Labour*

at *Montmartre,*
poets impaled on statues begged for inspiration
as the tourists watched the city lights, spark to fade
taking a thousand pictures
without pause.

The Thinker
saw *The Lovers' Hands* and *The Kiss*
in *The Moulin Rouge*
separately,
they reminded him of a *Headless and Handless Figure.*

He saw the cafe where,
Auguste Rodin met *Henri Rochefort*
turned into a Starbucks.

He saw the *The Walking Man* by Champs-Élysées,
the sale in Chanel veiling *The Tiredness* away,
he saw,
the Despair of selling Mona Lisa on postcards.

He saw *The Rich* walking up to Notre Dame
revealing *The Secret* to the poor
vagabonds reaching like *Hands Emerging From A Tomb.*

At night,
with a glass of wine
The Immortal Peasant thought of the good times,
when he grasped Paris's spirit and Rodin the artist,
he felt melancholic,
and shed tears of regret for the city he found,
before walking through his sculptor's *Gates Of Hell*
committing
an immortal suicide.

THE WATCHTOWER

She walks out on the street, shimmering in glitter,
sheltering the year's last thriller on her dark lips, under the snow
pouring a siege.

I shiver,
marooned atop the watchtower, voices of laughter flush down the spiral stairwell.
The night is in retreat under dayspring, like candlelight flaring.

The heavy gates shut behind her as if on the past,
reeling from the future.
Time can be heard counted down –
setting off a murky tug of war, between what's been and gone,
and the ever tightly isolated moment,
that had only just begun.

Cobbled streets spread parades below,
manifest as thousands of cold feet,
dragged through the confetti and the muddied snow –
I try and listen, through the festive commotion, to hear her steps
as she walks off, I shiver,
and when I hear no more, I give in and begin,
the early call for salvation,
like a crow, from this twisted minaret;
posed like an angel, petrified on a crypt,
surmounted,
by silent prayer.

HIGH ART

There's something about the texture
of this painting,
is it pointy or am I squinting? – "Really subdued."
Can I touch it? – "No."
"You know what you were just saying about the heart,
where the mark of any good work comes from?"
"I can't control how you look at my creations,
I'd have to get a chainsaw."
Stop, stop, stop
don't tell me, don't care.

Can art, as a fetish, catalyse intuition,
can it coagulate wisdom?
And who holds art's expertise?
Is that even a thing?
Maybe for its fetishists.

STIFF LIKE TREES WE GROW OLDER

Once supple as toddlers, like the pea green stem,
we were thick as thieves with our few leaves,
once, long before countless shed in the breeze.

Once humble hunchbacks, we curved for the light
our senses rooted in, delved out of sight.
We formed bulky, crusted bark
in seared layers over our warm blood,
and tirelessly swayed in its ebbs and tides,
as the bones calcified.

Shrouded like trees we grew older,
heavy on the shoulders – no more the receptive shape,
no more the eager reach.
Meanderings subsided at optimal heights.
We would've been fine without speech, finer perhaps
like the trees,
anchored further in a bit of our earth, every season, stretching the skin,
needing only a cup of water to grow within,
finding novelty even in the wind, creation in drifting pollen.

I remember the sky was closer, before I got taller,
when, like a sprout's spike through the earthly seed
I first looked up,
– life never before or again to feel so palpable –
like a baby or a tree at birth,
from the tried and the true,
moulded in mud, dreaming of the blue.

WARM UP

Tribute to London-born rave collective Warm Up

A heart-shaped neon flag waved above
a crowd loosely in sync
and it was no ordinary morning.
We slipped from the side of the stream,
down to the slopes in between
the road and the meadows, meeting under thick,
buzzing flow nets stretching,
bundled up, like sound, loaded in currents,
faster than bullets, adrift through the city's vessels,
pulsating through London's body.

Like electricity,
we too carry an unseen, unspoken, force
into our homes, often
quiet in the morning, quiet at night
everything and barely anything inside.
But here,
right underneath our thumping feet,
the dwellers of gargantuan towns,
something wakes in the restless earth,
something, pushing root and stem.
Reaching for that warmth we begin again,
to be convinced,
that this is more than "just a party",
or a carousel revolving
around its waxed fantasy.

Like any night that tears misconceptions apart
no one knows what they're doing or
who they are, necessarily,
the simple trick being that no one cares.

Music, movements and feelings alike,
often say more than boxes of words would like.
And show us how our eyes are stained
like our windows we seldomly clean.

As more and more of us found love,
in some form or another,
the more it mattered.
We mutated,
like fruits ripen overnight, over an hour
a moth reborn,
through a caterpillar's silken cradle,
trails to our roots reaching meaning,
in keeping alive.

We all had that image
carved in our sight,
that heart-shaped neon flag,
waving between, the earth and the sky
saluting Spring.
When the morning found us,
all curled up on the green grass,
staring in awe at the rays of dawn,
casting beauty as it swooned on and swept away.

The frost and calamity of darkness in retreat,
our tales bridged in a heartbeat,
nightly veils and masks cast as deceit,
rallied behind the wonder we screamed
like a moorland revived
over the sun soaring the sky
"now we rise!"

NED'S BRAGGARTS AND BEGGARS

Encased in a posh laced maze, just outside the Bank of England
I'm lost now with a beastly chow chow, that really doesn't like to be alone,
watching shadows come in and out of sight.
Walls rise steep over the city's sharp corners, entangling further into immemorable lanes.
I look over at a platinum blonde braggart, scolding a beggar passing by the smoking area,
Romanian melodies in her whistling, copper nickels jingling in her plastic cup.

The tip of a church bell, encased in a primitive gong, peeks over an ancient dome
and shrinks, towered by splitting, obsidian glass,
climbing to the heavens, racing a race that can only be against oneself.

Clocks carpet the velvet floors and the fancy
diamond striped cloaks fencing everyone's figure.
Time wasted as much as money, if not more.
Minutes trickle around coins tossed across the pavement, to reach an endless ditch to keep falling,
with no wishing well to settle in.
I gaze to the sharp-edged headlights of cars in traffic,
funnelling exhaust, tunnelling nowhere, jamming the streams of streets.

The braggart by the door sharpens her teeth with a pick,
dropping her chewed up gum into the beggar's cup, moving inside
sits on a stool, beside a ghostly man by the bar.
A hungered lustre in the eyes,
his hands touch up her ruby dress,
the chow chow yelps for help,
the crowd drools,
as Ned's braggarts loom
like moths to the night's lucent rays,
cheap replicas of the sun that pervades.

LADY LUCK

Lady Luck, it's early in the morning.
You're sleeping in your bed, and here,
I stroll awake,
awakened,
by dreams of your body under a lunar daze.
The salient passion in your fingertips,
like galleons sailing at dusk,
moves gently up my hands to my shoulder line,
your lips linger on mine like a Valium dream
and your kisses trace my skin warm,
like the sun's haze swimming.

Lady Luck, I hear echoes of thumping beats
and restless feet, dancing on a jagged lightning floor,
at the helm of modernity,
our archaic love moving bone to bone
nurtured amidst the numbing noise of the freak show.

Lady Luck, who am I to be when you wake up?
A pellucid light envelops the sky and veils faint stars.
I know I must fall to rest yet I know not how,
far from your easy laughter and
the wavelength of your breathing.
Lady Luck, meet me in the morning,
for now I long to love in a world you've carved
with your eyes in mine.

DEEP IN THE FOREST

Leather coats in meadows,
a carnival springs soul with sounds
spreading for miles like seas translated into rivers
translated into slow tides.

Unseen through the woods, a rift mends
between inside and out, like water
there is no external.
The rhythm that flickers across the puzzle
makes its pieces aware
that despite separate contexts,
they fit together perfectly.

And just when the walls come crumbling down,
we stare through the smoke clearing,
onto the rhythmic scene
and our primitive collective, shimmering,
some place forlorn somewhere along the tracks
that always felt alive when
we found each other.

The sunrise, shaping up the glares in eyes
took us by surprise,
piercing the moments we had come to question,
whether we chose to be aware,
like the earth before the first bud stemmed
or a song before its first note is struck.
A feeling of becoming, had we all not?

A saxophone sears into a phoenix,
in the music's spark
its wings wide like the rays of dawn

cutting through the viscous confusion of night,
crimson like a fuse alight
over barley burning,
lighting up the faces circling the sound in awe.

My body melts away as I lurk through the eyes
of infinite misfits
with currents forsaken beneath their feet,
arid stream beds meandering
to an ocean of calmed ripples
a future, that was once in reach.

A gentle mist veils the quivering of our back bones
laced against each other's,
resting on the bark of a fallen tree, you and me,
like birds preening,
under warm, distant frequencies reaching the earth's subtle skin.
We are falling, but like ashes,
dreaming we hover,
that we soar, that none but the wind will take hold,
that through each door, as our days so far proved
we'll return to the source,
the hallway of doors,
where we observe, where we watch,
not idle but alight
to feel the heat only to lead our steps back to the sleet
where we watch and learn alone
where for most of our lives we've preferred to return
to places forlorn along the tracks,
where we had always felt alive.

DANDELION (LION'S TOOTH)

Cornered by vinyl, sipping Southbank,
we watch the sleeping stream carry coloured reflections downtown.
Home astray on your Hellenic hair,
like a lantern juxtaposed with the leaking night.
Our wishful thinking, like the wind, shed dandelions – Lion's Tooth in Latin –

Life elsewhere manifest on your magnetic movements,
a silken spotlight on your dress, like a sunset
sinks from your shoulders down to your knees.
In a few hours, you're New York bound,
onto a jagged stage,
cloaked in smoke, your tale disguised,
the rail line a birthmark on your skin.

I lean in, and whisper "I'm sheltered"
in a glimpse of your clear blue arctic stratosphere,
when you turn to face me,
light through each droplet shines, from the crusts of ice in your eyes,
time, rendered barren right then,
a mammoth, unsullied in its frosted crest.

Nested in sharp contrasts, we sway to the music,
night sky scattered over your nails,
your fingers orbit the solar spin of the deck until we can hear the bells of St Paul's.
Our farewell, a hushed prayer,
a 70's gospel drapes your clicking heels,
I ghostly reach for your hand,
as if for the clock of a dandelion.

BLUE SKIES (LYRICS)

Eyes like blue skies
how can one keep from searching?
How far can I chase the light,
before dawn turns to night,
and heaven merges with hell?

Freed, freed, even for a moment when I stare
reeling from the twilight's tear
– like homecoming –
the sun long awaited, asleep,
rising.

Eyes like blue skies
the dark extinguished in its hue, do I believe, can it be true?
I'm to blame, I lay my palms bare,
and sang this prayer,
answered in the open plains, delivering
a woman June brings.

Then cherry blossoms blushed,
the brightness started to last
later and later into eventide,
I held onto your blue skies
far from my anchor to the earth.

After the frost
my skin shed, my chances crossed,
I thought I'd die here in the dark,
the cauldron of this dome, this crucible of war
then a knock on my door, you out of the blue
just enough to get me through

like the world's asylum
from a cosmic vacuum!

You, the blue!
Take me with you, when you go with that rising moon
when heaven's merging with hell
where everything is reborn,

I'll disappear with you and the sun,
I'll run.

IN THE SHADOW OF AN EMPIRE

Caged in a rectangular city square,
hemmed in by ancient bells and arch symbols
of bricks and cement,
cold, efficient beliefs stand tall.
Almost as tall as the flags that
sway nonchalantly, towering over the figures below,
common demands coated in white lies,
deified, crossed with blood.
Though barely seen as such by the eyes of passers-by,
along these wide boulevards.

Along these manicured streets cloaked in oak and sycamore
bells echo into the growing darkness, no one heeds them anymore.

And the strong wind that travelled the world around and around
returned having heard it all
but couldn't tell
carrying leaden clouds on its back
which covered the blinding sun
foretold once not to set,
and the mood of a grey afternoon
settled on the wetland.

HEADING DOWN SOUTH

A busted bus, engine clustering,
sways side to side from its overload.
I'm heading down South again.
"As South as you can get" the conductor says
and if I'm lucky, I may even get time to go down to the sea,
to be just across the coast from home,
closer, yet so far still.

Chilling winds blow out on the narrow road,
withered branchlets of trees lash against my top deck window,
like flashbacks of memories
the cold starts sinking its teeth in
and I'm speeding, down South again
near where grandma's last days await by a fireplace,
with a longing ablaze.
I want to ask her what she keeps from saying,
and how much it hurts,
the crackling skin.

Lights are up all over the towns passing by,
candles in church halls kindle hope,
flickering to resurrect saints into shadows
through coloured windows.

A moth trapped inside the bus,
wanders up and down, left and right,
any which way it knows it can go,
tangled in shifting, opaque lights shining
from the other side of the glass.
Through the journey, it spends its time
biting through tears
in the thick curtains, to no end.

The rain is now battering the ceiling,
the bus, with its dimmed floor lights,
speeds in the quicksand of darkness.
Some are asleep, some are dazed, scrolling shiny screens,
a few seem to be reading,
and something brews in my bones, my sinews, my marrow –
the nostalgia of yesterdays
and that of tomorrow
then I remember. That we split,
the embodiment of each other; my home and me.
Like how, in a station's crowd, one is but a speck,
yet on the road becomes the focus, the sole subject.

I'm heading down South, the conductor says "as south as you can get"
and if I'm lucky, I may even get time to be by the sea,
just across the coast from home; where all are born half forlorn,
if they hold on at all. And after all the years and tears undue,
in my country, my abyss where most doors lead,
looking back I'll regret only,
to have known so few,
and walked by so many.

SLEEPER TRAIN

The moon is up,
slip sliding its silver blend down on the steel sleeper
cutting across the tracks.

The famished cold chews at the train's stove
and my chest bones.
From the windows of the wagon's bed,
the earth is a composition
of successive images speeding past my head,
continuously overlapped.

The passengers are too old to be right,
too young to be sincerely in self-doubt.
The stars no less bewildering as they travel
the sun no brighter.
The riddle is cursed, for who seeks a final answer,
what are we really after?

I'm almost done with my time here,
I mean, trailing across the plains, conquering fear.
I'm convinced this is the way it had to be,
when I uttered a silent prayer:
God is waiting, his shepherd the sands of time,
my body the Grim Reaper –

Most are afraid on this train, afraid of something,
though they often seem nonchalant,
fear is rife, though for some it seems to seep into everything but,
it is a trap this train,
eventually leading to the very thing we've been holding off.
I keep hope close, but like Desmond Tutu,
"a prisoner of hope,"

to catch the next Spring back home
in time for all the weddings, before all the facetimed
funerals –
yes I believe still and am bound to until
cemeteries shed their flowers.

Though time seems to calm on whirling wheels,
numbing, in a ceaseless, circular motion –
It's just an illusion for us passengers
to delay, the decay for another day, another dollar –

I feel this, so I'm restless,
pacing through the long, eerie corridors.
Where at each step, the floorboards move
and I can't sleep on the sleeper train.

Looking for someone, like a destination,
like words on my tongue, elusive again,
as the train speeds on, cutting through the night
to another wakeful dawn.

9999 NAILS

Specks of time are dispersed
through the freckles in your face to space.
Space, that flickered open
beneath a single shot fired,
planets spit down like
irascible gunpowder.
And far from this eternal war above our heads
we take cover from our own,
in that shack of a flat we shivered under, two teenagers
night upon night, ticking clocks under the sheets
cuddling the lie that we've found shelter.

All this and more boxed up,
in a single cube of sugar I drop in a cup,
you call it a bitter Americano,
I call it cyanide.
I take you through each sip, hand in hand,
frail yet jubilant
"you have much to learn" you whisper.
You say I'm too young,
you say I'm not there,
you say I've never been,
you scream, sip, scream and sip,
you say you'll make do.

All this time I follow an ancient premonition.
I lay awake each night on a bed of ten thousand nails,
with 9999 pulled carefully apart but the one,
screwed up right against my heart.
Never pressing winds are the masquerades of life,
but shallow fingertips of oceans translated into rivers,
translated into slow tides,

never too soon is the final embrace,
the grounding of our great flight.
You must know we truly and rightfully reached the top,
but neither of us could've known
how closely it would come to resemble
the bottom of a stained cup.

"Another!" you raise your hand in despair
and I deny it to you,
first an Americano
then a kiss, then words.
The silence
reaches out to wrap its arms around you in comfort
for all that's said and done
yet you push it back, with an arrow of a slap
and a whisper, that may well have been a scream.
"Why?" you ask,
the question mark ripples in specks of time
dispersed through freckles in your face to space.
Each beat of the heart now encapsulated in the void
and set apart,
like planets flushed in gunpowder waiting to spark,
with no hero, no sunset and no iron vest forthcoming
for the love lost,
till eternity and all the rest.

I'M A POET

I

I *am* the Tower of Babel, I live in all the languages.
They say translations ruin poetry
but I've seen words transform to find a new home in any land, on any tongue.
I'm a shiver, my voice a quiver, from emptiness around the heart,
encased in chest bones rattling.
Often my best company are the names and faces I can't see,
readers who often feel distanced to me and from each other.
Since the good lord split our speech apart,
least that's how the legend goes,
I speak the sentences some won't dare utter to others.

In the state of our societies, I'm honoured to say,
I am part of the resistance for the many against the few,
the compassionate, vulnerable people, tangled in a webwork of envy, strangled
under dictatorial authority,
or the lonely, the disenchanted, the blinded. I resonate with all and one.

I strive in rhyme though I try to stray.
I summon intricate views from idle sights
though I can't make them stay.
If a wave undulated in someone's eyes,
you could see by my certainty,
for poetry can be a dictionary of details all can see
but rarely come to speak.

II

Us poets, gathered here in the dark,
all our finest dreams clenched tight in our fists,
our pens sharp as spears, like gladiators we have come from all corners of the world
to the grand arena that is language,

encircled by spectators cheering for our demise!
Defying twisted treadmills turning for ages past,
we forewarn the young of their aggrieved grind, before their innocence dies.

I'm a poet and I'm never blinded
to the light that lit the world.
I learned that I can build bridges or burn them in writing
even make or break worlds in words,
which shift seamlessly in meaning,
by who's listening.

Though they may be intangible or inhabitable
and may slip through your fingers like castles of sand,
the assembly of words is inevitable still,
their territory impossible to conquer or besiege.
For they breathe a form of life that outlives me,
for as long as anyone can speak, there'll be poets
for most of us, as Sait Faik said, would go crazy if we weren't writing.

I'm a poet and I ask of you
not to dwell on what I meant and what I can never say,
even I am oblivious, split from my piece
forever when it's finished.
And I'm unable to explain why it exists
any more than why anything else does,
though I still keep looking for a way,
to show what I'm seeing, in these images,
that by no stretch only reveal themselves to me.

I'm a poet!
I *am* the Tower of Babel.
Though you may not speak my tongue,
all can share in the awe at our imagined shrines,
encased in images and feelings prevalent well beyond our time.

Language, built on the shoulders of giants,
carries me gallantly,
as the future scatters out of my hands
into notebooks for me to find many years down the line.
They wheel memories along, like a train's rails over time's rust.
Pages pile, revealing their truth once disguised.

I'm an unforgiven forgiver,
I am a designated driver drunk on the wheel.
I derive fantasies out of monotony, though it still gets to me.
I make monuments of moments, though not of stone, towering over
      from where we cannot be,
but in words on the contrary, permeable like water
passing through bodies.

I wish above all to nurture my community, those around me
as I do the sparrows, tossing handfuls of breadcrumbs,
I too shouldn't be so needy; peanuts make elephants happy.

I'm a poet
and I cut right through my boredom and cynicism,
with poorly scribbled lines, like an ant's prayer as we say in Turkish.
Behind my desk, on a train, on a plane, sometimes nauseating
like on a rocking boat but I try and stay afloat over any sullen reproach.
A labourer for human rights, nine to five,
like a coast guard, armed with a spoon against tsunamis,
when I too need saving from drowning.

I'm a poet and like many I too am broke.
But I can still grow to contain any imagery not lost on me!
I can encircle fascists and their fearful armies,
I wouldn't think twice to take in refugees or
the shrill shrieking of people haunted by pain
and lovers torn in vain, are all welcome,
I'll make space for them to stay forever.

I'll expand to embrace them
and attempt getting to know myself.

III

Even though we are burning,
us poets, at least we are aware of it.
Unlike the frog in a boiling pot
nerves sheared by the heat
taking its cauldron for a jacuzzi
slowly dying in deceit.

I fear not being a tiny part of a vast enigma!
After all "to merge with the whole is a great consolation" said Seneca,
one of our finest colleagues.

I'm a poet, so by default a lover.
As love chants charting, one long trail from heart to heart,
moulded by all into mine, beating obstinately on.
I persist in the pursuit of love, one place or another.

I'm a poet,
and I don't subscribe to the destitute views on the TV,
I take a bird's eye perspective
on war turned grief, love turned longing,
forgetting to remembrance, etc
I look upon everyone leaving to stay behind,
dichotomies are rife in the realm of poetry, as in life.

And when I see others of my kin, fellow poets,
our eyes meet, like sharp headlights on a deserted road,
we read each other's lines and sweep past similar paths as we travel on,
swallowed by the dark wasteland,
the journey getting the better of us.

There's much I will not know and many I'll never meet,
but within the ability to concede, I find
lies a peace.
To ease determinist convictions over what anything may be.

I'm a poet and poets are sewing machines,
makeshift repairers of a torn human fabric.

In any tug of war I'm the rope,
I tend to dwell on crossroads,
for there's something restless, almost
obscene in new faces, wandering strangers
I cannot judge in a simple brush nor stay listless.

I'm a poet who cannot be imprisoned, though many have tried,
over walls and barbed wires I can seamlessly take flight
like a frail kite.

I'm quick to call out a cruel crowd when I see one,
or a circus of clowns cheering for a lion's leap
through a circle ablaze, the brave being framed and tamed?
I won't stand for that.
But still as a poet, I refuse to build walls around myself
or anywhere else for that matter,
I refuse to hold grudges,
against the sinful or the scoundrel who also frequent my pages,
to atone for their mistakes or to take my stretched out hands
to do what they must,
and burn me at the stake for us both to bite the dust.

My fellow poets in the dark, it's not that long ago
that we were hunted down,
and some of us are still,
but we've been banished to the shadows long enough,
so I'm here to tell you that

today will be different, tomorrow will be the same.
And that I'm leaving.
You're free to come along but grab your coat,
for here, somehow, it's always raining.

I'm a poet, often the town crier
for the changing of seasons
and change within.
I keenly observe time's subtle work,
I see windows of meaning narrowing.
The world turned upside down,
a broken youth dancing on barren fields
with feelings anesthetized.

IV

I know after all that life is just one life that I come to know.
That my reality is entrenched by my body, a certain mentality.
Still I hold true, that everything comes from the outside much as in,
and keep my eyes, ears and heart open.

It's equally likely for anyone to read, so I keep writing
about the endless circles around which we live,
sleeping to wake, eating to defecate,
consuming to make, tidying to clean, day in, night out.
Can't we break this cycle, I ask,
this wilful slavery that punctured into our body postures?
It is far past time to make amends, my friends!

I swayed like you in our cradles and swings
and I too have grown older, don't be fooled that I'm still young.
I oscillate with you these days on the pendulum of delirium.
As the greed of the masses makes reckless claims on what's not ours,
in nature's grief and love, and the eternal night and light,
I salute you!

Though the creator split our languages,
we poets couldn't be kept from carrying the ladders of words,
making way from mudbrick debris
to Babylonian heavens.

BEING MISSING

I was missing,
myself and lots of other things,
but then I found,
what was lost like what was gained
ever remained.

This is the reality of everything,
if I don't get to keep nothing, so be it.
It doesn't matter, because we've got the spirit;
that will never grow older, I will never miss a beat.
Never lose sight of the journey behind.
It's up to you to choose life as a state of mind
and I refuse to think it's all lost and gone.
This is a moment to shine and remember that
everything that's been and done
is always here, forever and now
and I love life and I love death and everything that comes
after it
'cause I'm glad to be here and that's it.

DEDE (GRANDPA)

I

When the fuck knows I can finally return home,
I fear to find my grandpa's photos, instead of him.

The curtains drawn in his living room, dust piled on brittle
chandeliers which were majestic jewels to me as a kid.
Hanging from the ceiling, veiled by embroideries. His
resounding laughter frozen in frames on the walls, wrapped
by the silence, sunk in the house, the grandfather clock still
ticking.

I fear to find the scent of his sharp cologne gone,
no more the sound of his rustled breaths that I'd hear
hurling, sleeping on his chest;
small things that back then I couldn't understand,
made a home for me to remember, no matter where I am.
So I remind myself; it's not the dying that matters. Having
lived together, once and forever
thereafter.

II

My grandpa would spend hours by his windows, eagerly
waiting on us to visit, watching the road with jaded
eyes. Our arrival was more than enough to make his day,
later his weeks and later his numbered months in longer
stretches; life was busy for us, his younger ones, though
we'd try to come around often as we could.

I could never have thought that we would be ripped apart,
turned into outcasts and that I would be miles away,

standing in his shoes by my windows, now waiting for
him to come to me. Too far from his place in Ankara, I
sit trying to gather the pieces of what remains. It stings, it
aches from my toes to my fingertips, watching elders and a
homeland slip away like this, from a distance.

Yearning, like a rusted blade, cuts nearer to the gut, I feel
helpless with nothing to do, defenceless with all I've got.

III

My dearest grandparents... My wise, tender elders, loved
us in infinite abundance. Once, they were younger than
the morning, they were ways ahead. They ran the longest
marathon any of us had, to get my parents and I a decent
education. In front of their own stern folks, they couldn't
even cross their legs out of respect, but in us they found
love more than they ever had around. They nurtured my
days, my walk, my talk. Once, they captained the ship.
Of our lineage. They steered us through the pilgrimage
of our ancestry. And now in the wintertime of their lives,
they wait sunken in armchairs by the wide windows. Frail
and grey, they pray in quiet beds to catch the sunrise, their
shortening breaths and fickle memories once again.

IV

I'm a refugee and what that means is,
I haven't seen my grandparents, any other elders
or family members for the past six years.
Some, are on the brink of death and I shiver in fear
of facetimed final words. It hurts. When no words
but a single touch can say it all, to be denied from it.
I should prepare yet I shudder, like a stray dog in winter.

Like a sinful believer, when I hear the voice of a Muezzin,
calling morning's prayer over us all stranded,
between night and day, life and death.

I can't go back but I never really left either, my heart beats
ever closer to a home afar.

My Grandpa, one of my creators, he always said
we would all turn to dirt and dust. But I disagree, I must.
I can feel him now, I can still hear him
walking with me, living, in me all along.

V

I started writing after my Grandpa who passed away, Ali Rıza,
who never got to see me graduate,
but it reminded me so bitterly of the one who lives still,
Hüseyin, so far out of my reach,
slipping into murky memories; amnesia's abyss,
losing touch with us and the rest of his life.

As a baby, early at the crack of dawn
he would take me on a stroller to long walks by the sea,
so I could catch fresher breaths.
He was a forester much of his life and I dreamt
of the two of us, deep in the woods last night;
he carried towering trees on his back and planted them firm in
the earth,
as I painted budding flowers on their branches.

The first word I ever uttered was "dede"
which means "grandpa" in Turkish.
He always looked at me, the way a sculptor would at his art,
through his kindness and faith, he took me in as a baby,
leapt up on his feet whenever he saw me, arms wide open

with love, like the gates of Zion
calling me, "The prophet's lion!"
as I learnt, on his knees,
that no distances nor death will outreach,
our togetherness.
Like how through the sun's passage, the moon gets kindled;
so we all come to pass, by the hands of our elders beloved.

PROVIDES

Cowritten with James Dowsett[5]

We're engraved in the cosmic, wheeling rhythm
riding our own pace of time
– that is divine, in the eternal rhyme –
we abandoned ourselves to the skies
the horizons of fiction and association,
prototypes and pigments flushed out,
crawling through the looking glass
our eyes seeing past,
we follow the same journey as anybody, really
from inside to out and back in, that's where the train is
heading.
But meandering, losing the way to finding it,
delving into the fragile, derelict archives of the mind
that provides.

5 Thanks to James for permission to publish this poem in this collection.

WORSHIP STREET

On the old town square, I sit on the steps of a church
beside a beggar half-asleep against its gates shut,
watching the passers-by on the street.
– Worship Street to be exact –
I contemplate the solitude, deeply.
Having a suicidal cigarette, seeing
the filthy rich on a senseless spree,
spending everyone's chances.
Youths drift by drunken minds,
people pass by with pets and bikes, bags,
tennis rackets and tracksuits
all on a mission, rushing,
the old timers, ambling, paying attention to their steps,
dreaming of softer bedsheets.

In the heart of hipster land,
monstrous advertisements hang over our heads,
for deals better than dignity. Ceaseless constructions,
strange architectures, rise over the city,
the tomb stones of titans
towering over the crumbs of our figures.

Burdened attention spans dwell on banknote threads
like fishes on a hook, pulled,
by accountants book keeping
by complexes, cloaked in mirrors.
Foucault's panoptical eye, up a furnace
watches over the cells of individuals,
the prisoners of the self.

There is a small book shop, on Worship Street,
next to fast food carts selling fry ups.

There are people wearing their watches
where their hearts should be
on their sleeves,
passing by in a hurry, failing to notice things.
People kissing each other in the rain,
opportunists selling umbrellas,
phone contracts and pocket-sized politics.

By nightfall, above and below
the celestial scenery and the street's misery are
superimposed.
I still hide from being seen,
until someone spots me eventually
and with the same puzzled look stares back at me,
and for a second we fathom,
how to be all alone and all together.

There are people who I am, and whom are a part of me.
After all, we *are* the people that suffered for us.
So I choose to pull down the curtains
on my complexes in mirrors.

Me and the rough sleeper keep to our seats,
by the church on Worship Street;
me still under the spell, him in the vicinity,
of humanity.
We don't speak or ask why
and just wait on the side-lines, for the hammer to fall.
Our prayers are whispered,
and we are unsure as ever,
if we want someone to answer the call
or if we want the answer at all.

ANY FENCE

I know I won't be here for long,
because I won't belong
on either side of any fence,
as time blurs, breaching the boundaries
of my sense of self.

WHEN IT'S OUR TURN

Written following the tragic deaths of two musicians İbrahim Gökçek and Helin Bölek, both members of Grup Yorum, a band frequently prosecuted in Turkey for their revolutionary music branded as terrorist propaganda. Read İbrahim Gökçek's last article at The Morning Star *titled "I used to be a guitarist, now I'm a terrorist" to find out more about his plight. This poem was performed as part of the solidarity series "Creative Witnesses".*

Dedicated to the giants upon whose shoulders we all live

The giants of my homeland, freedom fighters in all corners of the world,
I won't ever settle for defeat,
thanks to you,
burgeoning enlightenment upon it!
Those that grow like bittersweet vines, the stubborn masters
born into the aching destinies of our geographies.

Those who carved one out of none,
the solid crews of swaying ships thrusted,
like pendulums across opposite shores...
The bright souls of our past,
in a choir I hear them,
their voices ring in our ears.
Us: still petulant, sombre and forgetful.
Them: as if by each passing day,
bolder, braver and more insistent –
Their minds, strings and words still mightier than the swords
pistols and whips that lashed at their backs.

Those who nourished our minds, our hearts
and these lands we call home tirelessly, against its cruelty.
Those who fostered humanity and carved the sun's light for it,
you, the giants, upon whose shoulders I rose and could walk.

"I mean the likes of you:
Nazım Hikmet, Deniz Gezmiş, Hrant Dink, Uğur Mumcu,
İsmail Hakkı Tonguç, Metin Altıok, Hasret Gültekin,
Lui Xiabo, Victor Jara, Perhat Tursun, İbrahim Gökçek..."

Generation after generation, the deliverers of enlightenment
were taken by beating,
for emboldening the minds of the many,
they often departed too early, to the dreaming of our hearts.
This poem is for them.

You endured for your right to the truth,
and when it's my turn
I will stand upright just alike. Head held high, I will follow your lead.

When it's my turn,
to rise against injustice,
to remember the lives lost in vain, to understand them with coming age,
when it's my turn like it was once yours,
I will proudly shoulder my past,
get wrapped up in the history of my country,
and wider human family
and invite the silenced, to speak up on my tongue.
When it's my turn,
I will not be cowed, just like you were not.
Innocent lives not spared for the love they had,
for all that never loved them back.

When we get our share of this recklessness,
when it's our turn to pay the dues,
we will strive to be worthy of your memory.
You have not been forgotten.
We will rattle the walls deemed impenetrable
from the underground,
by the roots of olive trees, nurtured eternally.

Alas the brothers and sisters of my generation,
of future generations.
We loved you so dearly, each of you, like family
and now you call out to us in the crowds,
with the words of old Italian revolutionaries,
"You must bury me with your hands,
take me to your land" [6]

When it is our turn
to embrace your brightness,
we will spring hope for generations,
breaking from our halters,
we will gallop to each other's help,
with the strike of a brush,
with the sound of a piano, a guitar,
we will prove one can be happy to live still.

One must live,
but humanely, this is what you all told me
and it seems that in this country,
what falls on us is always to be late,
to the brightest minds,
to the bravest hearts
to the best of youths,
always late to care.

With your struggle, writers' pens sharpened
to inscribe humanity upon history.
To anyone with a shred of conscience
left in their chests,
in one breath you all couldn't take,
you bestowed unison,
you didn't leave us alone, even at death.

6 lyrics of 'Bella Ciao'

Oh you, the brave hearts of this universe!
You bent prison bars,
you ripped apart the fear of love from hearts,
you shook up conscience,
conquered minds my brothers and sisters,
you bestowed a family to the orphaned!

As we struggled only to live,
you, from the beating, muck and mud,
moulded humanity and pulled it out
from the guts of bitter ideologies.

They keep saying
"art doesn't die, neither music, or literature",
they keep saying,
but it's people and their stories that are immortal,
people, beating on in every heart,
against all that tries to make it stop.

What's immortal is love,
is light.

Now it's my turn, my masters!
The turn of our generation, to hold up your banners.
Go in peace,
reconcile with the beautiful souls dearly departed.
Your vigilance, you should know is safe with me, with us.

On the shores of darkened seas, your watch
on cynical dinner tables, your words,
upon time, your mark
you should know is safe with me, with us.

Bless you all!

We know well that a half-hearted life is lived in vain,
we know that if only fears are defeated
the struggle will be well worth it!

Now it's my turn, all over again.
It's a sad affair under the stars but we are not alone,
when we truly, fall in love.

TIME THAT SPENDS (LYRICS)

Time that spends and makes amends,
rotted on the road and now you reprimand,
where we are,
and where we've been
seems to be the answer over everything,
so make up your mind.

Those that don't,
heed it not.
Seeking truth or seeking lies
don't hide behind, those sweet eyes
cast up from the wood,
when she brings the rain again,
take the signs you understand
and make up your mind,
make up your mind.

Being perplexed, between two things, kills,
any choice trumps indecision –
(even and sometimes especially the wrong one)

– where we are and where we've been
seems to be the answer over everything,
so make up your mind.

If my fingers could trace
the shores of your face,
I'd show you what time abrades
while the sun is still your rising grace, embrace,
me and all the rest of this world,
and make up your mind
go brave into the night
and make up your mind.

It's time that spends and makes amends
what was murky now turns sublime –
the sanctity of life, if there is one,
truly shines
when you wake up, take a look around
and make up your mind.

TO VICTOR AUDERA, THE GREAT

In just three months, my brother's father was swept away
by cancer, it swallowed him whole as he shrivelled in his
body like an olden tree, before he passed it all on, to Victor
Audera the Great, Third of his name.

The Great, because evolution, on its leaden shoulders,
carried his sturdy mind and body firmly, furthest to this
pinnacle of development that is my friend, when you think
about it. To its most sharpened point, like a sculpture in the
making, encapsulating a family history. Through evolution,
generation after generation, the DNA, characteristics
and physical traits transfigured, from face to face, Victor
Audera from his dad from his grand-father before him, his
time had come to yield the torch, with a burning passion to
persist long as the pump through the heart, gushing blood.

"So long as you remember and so long as you breathe" I
say over the phone "in you, your blood, your genes, your
love, Victor Audera, the Great, shall live on, the titanic title
passed on, from father to son.

You, now, are him, and those long before him. Who have
been and gone. Like those endless circles you kept telling
me, that Marquez was writing of."

It took a lot of death to keep us all alive, it occurs to me
suddenly. "Remember the dead, through the wake of
the living, remember the trails in memories, stretching
back to learning how to tie your laces." Remember, that
consciousness surely travels beyond death, through the
shoulders and souls of giants we stand on. There is a river,
that separates, the living and the dead. Though passage is

bizarre it's far, from one way only, there are countless bridges
on which we still meet, like melancholy, dreams and reveries,
with our dear departed, us the meek, shattered or sheltering still,
under life's fated defeat.

So what's next for Victor Audera, the Great?

Well, it begins where it ends.
Like currents pushed and pulled by the moon, on the move until
all our seamless heights are summoned, back to the source, the
force, gravitas.
We must be grateful to how special it all was, to have been who
we are.
And Victor Audera, the Great
is and will ever be too, whenever he reunites with that which he
seeks to find, within.

Victor Audera, the Great is here still.
There, in my brother's eyes. His curious look through the
windows of his car as he speeds up past those places we once
called home and grew up in, listening to "whatever we want"
eating, saying, playing and running from whatever, we wanted.
And though we may never relive those exact moments,
in our search to find whatever,
they will always be inscribed in our struggle to live.

Victor Audera, the Great, is not fallen
but rising your perfect past and its shimmering moments,
are yours ever still.

You are carrying the torch honourably on, the way he walked,
the way you learned to talk on his knee and the way you both
were just always kids inside. How you both learnt to come to
show others like me too, just how to live, to challenge a sense of
defeat, that so long as you love from the heart, you can do:
"Whatever you want" –

That dark green majestic jeep, we were speeding in, on our way
to school now buried deep in our childhood, now seems like an
allegory. For the fertile freedom gifted by our family, upon our
playful grin, still remaining.

The way your father slammed the pedal, harking down the clear
highway, when he picked us up. The way he turned the sound all
the way up and got us engulfed in hard rock, was you exactly.

What's next for Victor Audera, the Great?

I know that's a question you can only ask yourself.
But in the men who carried the same name I see no big distinction,
and I know the dignified person now in front of me
will walk that extra mile for them both, for eternity.

And Victor Audera, the Great, will evermore remain as one great
man,
living and growing in gratitude and respect in my heart.

ONE QUARTER

The moon is a quarter of the way through,
the rest carrying what it can't yet show you.

On the rise, it renders the black obsolete,
and the blue, concealed in icy hues.
At each invisible step, shades of the yellow sheds,
a kind impossible to forget.
Hark! In a few breaths,
that too recedes,
and the moon seems a stained medallion, skeletal white,
tied around the neck of night,
it climbs, shape shifting
like skin stripped to bone
like the light in a pair of eyes gone
like a dream, a monument in its heights forlorn
like being gradually unborn.

The moon is a quarter of the way through
the rest carrying what it can't yet show you.

IMPARADISED

An incalescent whiz, from afar,
whispers into the ear of a common fly.
The sound nearly the same buzz as his,
it beckons with luminescence,
flashing on his wings
dizzying his head,
dazzling his eyes.
The fly turns ceaselessly around, fearlessly
many a time. At each round
the closer he gets
to that grand lamp, the more
it enchants his mind.

It seems like a sun of gold, a mystical temple for the fly
though he hurts the more he nears,
and keeps knocking his head against the walls of glass
he doesn't desist,
because the blindness of darkness lays heavy
once enlightenment catches your eyes.

Finding a chink at last
when he slips in to the luminaire,
he starts to understand
as his nerves are fried like eggs on a pan
that paradise of light he hoped to find
is but a field of cadavers.

IS IT YOU OR IS IT THE LONGING?

Is it you or is it the longing,
the sincerity in simple things?
The cycle of days on repeat
but like sex, anew at each turn,
a pinnacle of pleasure perpetually peaking?

Is it you or is it the longing,
there, outside my window,
the figure of a woman walking past,
carrying groceries,
when she looks up and I can almost see her smiling?

In two sparrows too,
I wonder if it's the longing I am seeing, or you,
peeling feathers on the wings, rowing through winter's bitter winds,
soaring after each other and into a nest of a tree's withered branchlets,
disappearing.

When, despair comes certain, and the burden of living seeps deep
"you fool" I think, it can only be the longing.

Yet, I catch my eyes fixed at the doors sometimes, or even a crucifix
looking for you still;
to amble in, meandering,
like the ebb and flow – you come and you go,
this much perhaps I could settle for
if I stopped asking myself, is it you or the longing that makes me feel so,
convinced to hope on.

When I'm awakened by creaking on my wooden floors,
in the frozen light of a winter's moon, I think of you
caught between dream and sleep I almost feel you,

wandering the hollow hall.
I sit up waiting for the honeycomb light to seep under the door,
yet it remains dark.

Should I carry or be leaving
the belief that there is a meaning?
Perhaps the women passing by outside
and the crows that nestled in dead branches hide
are all but signs, that there's something between you and the longing
an everlasting state of mind,
heeding, the epitaph of loving
like echoes of distant bells, tolling.

A PLAYFUL DAY'S END

Growing up,
like a playful day's end,
left us all stranded,
some too quick to seek, some too late to hide.

ANOTHER YEAR

And here I am still
less of myself,
yet somehow evermore.

AFTER DECEMBER

It seems like a story of our own, too often cut too short,
these Christmas trees laid out on the side of the roads.
From love to lack of love, bought and sold
crowned cornerstones of warm homes,
for a sight of beauty to behold.

Dolled up in detail, best bib and tucker put on,
coiled up in bright wired lights head to toe,
only to be stripped back out to dried branchlet bones
dragged down the stairs and thrown out alone,
like a disowned chaperone,
into the new year's twilight zone.
Much like the ways
many people give praise to their Lord.

NEW YEAR'S MORNING (LYRICS)

I

It's 6 am on New Year's morning
and I sit by a dimmed corner light,
as it snows on an olden Berlin,
the grand oak in the courtyard shed naked to skin,
like her by my bedside, the feelings within –
days that end to begin with our whispering,
like paper lantern stars, hung all around in the wind.

The night breaks apart
through the window I gaze into myself,
ghostly layers blurred on the glass,
just out of reach, as if to profess –
My reflection too now comes to pass,
disappearing as the day breaks fast,
free, free at last!

I wonder right then,
why I'm up at this early hour.
Wasted and tired, the truth transpired
and she sleeps, next to me
like a yellow tulip
by the sun-like gates of the next few days,
where I too may find I'm at home.
Then why do I sit here alone?
Like a broom my guitar, sweeping yesterday by,
they say "don't go living in the past"
but to me it all feels made to last.

II

Though these are not the words I wish to sing,
they break out my chest, put to rest, nonetheless
for there is something to find at this hour,
a solitude but like the womb, I confess.
Hear from me, a voice defiant of life's contempt,
I'll always be alone at this hour.
Longing this way or the other, cause you don't have to,
my sister, my brother,
I wish none had to wonder if they were loved at all –

Like the lacklustre lavender,
on my balcony in the cold
hanging by threads in winter's crest,
so in poems they may spring and spring,
and to lapels get pinned and pinned!

I tried to keep a wider eye, tried to be yours or mine
tried to be blind, tried to understand why,
there's no forsaking that clear old sight,
that fight for a promise, that's sure kept alive,
although it passes through a hermit's state of mind.
I see now, that's the price, for tenderness to get by,
as these early mornings with their shadows and fears
play on my unwieldy young years –

they leave behind dark circles around the eyes,
a disguise,
for a scorpion's suicide, when surrounded by the flame,
its freedom ever proclaimed.

AFTER THE FOREST & THE FIRE WERE GONE

I

I'll admit I was left alone,
after the forest and the fire were gone.
I worked the fields night till dawn.
Storm in the distance,
rain on the rye.
I was right to leave the front
but I was left to bear being alive,
to wait for the sun to leave and arrive
for life to pass, remembrance by.

I didn't get to choose, this tussle with time,
to refuse
tomorrow is senseless
today is to be confused.
Every person, every place is a chapter –
meaning is to recollect, the moment is excused.

II

Can you hear my plea?
Or remember who you were?
I sometimes remember who I was, walking on the beach,
looking at the pieces of coloured glass, crushed in the sand
years on end, crusted, losing edge
and still shining in the sun yet, like beautiful gems.
Perhaps prettier in softened pieces then they ever were
artificially put together.

Work up the courage to falter,
to be melancholic, to rust!
No, the years won't be kind to us.

There was a fire, now there's a storm,
so here are some heavy stones, dear friend, would you like some more?
To anchor you down?
Tie them to your ankles carefully,
when the tempest hits at last, they'll keep you steady.
As an Arabic saying goes, losses make the riches.

Do you see now what I'm trying to do?
Do you see the clues?
I'm just here, waiting for you.
I hear that you are growing colder too,
won't you hold these cold hands?

CLOCKTOWER

I

People in the park turn around the clocktower.
Kids to adolescents,
grown men to old men.
Orbital, walking to grow and shrink.
It's a fascinating ordeal, to witness and to think
about just what defines the pace
of the many circles they endlessly thread.

Yet I swear you can see, around this here clocktower,
through the people turning eternally around it,
how all the circles track such delicate parallels.

Pushed and pulled, to and from one another, like planets the people
move side to side a while,
experiencing togetherness in speed, in a joint rotation, however long it lasts
before drifting apart to their own solitary circles in space, their own pace of time.

It's the clock itself I don't understand,
why it stands at all and why so tall...
And why are we all here endlessly turning around it
till our joints get rusted, knees and bones torn to shreds
skin shrinking and reveries forlorn, we turn and we turn
so seamlessly in harmony.

I wonder about the past and those who were left behind,
doing the old rounds around this tower of time.
I can sense their bodies, fallen along the tracks
slim bones reaching forward –
though I can't see them, I feel them in the earth, layered and stacked
as inscribed on a piece of rock further ahead,

"soil had passed and will again pass
every few years, through the bodies of worms"[7]

I can't stop to ask when does it all end and when did it start,
this charade of birth and loss?

II

I am here, as a visitor. Left my home in a Byzantine summer, a
violet afternoon, not a clue I wouldn't be returning anytime soon.
They called it a post-coup crackdown; I watched the Reichstag
Fire all over again. Lives getting torn under a dictatorship, blame
spewed and scattered like broken glass bits. As a country, we were
tormented by the collective guilt, it spilled.

All suffered except for the disciples of Sisyphus, everyone lost their
minds or went blind somewhat. I witnessed the mightiest wills of
my parents' generation broken and the sweetest hearts shattered,
the kindest faces tormented. Riches plundered and trust ravaged
by corrupted savages. I felt home, like parts of my body, get
dismembered into pieces. I couldn't bear the brokenness, so I forced
myself to believe all was ever intact. Where would I be without that
belief?

III

Around this clocktower, we are all juxtaposed in the moment,
yesterday and now, the why and the how – I remember that *we* are
alive and many lost their lives, ways and hearts – I remember all the
faces rendered chalk white, from agony of all kinds.

I rose shelters from my memories of home, when hurt, I carried it
gallantly, like a torch sprung against the dark, like flowers laid in
graveyards.

7 Quote by Charles Darwin found inscribed on a stone at London's Caledonian Park

There was no way to see back then, the longing to come from within. As I searched with hungered eyes, the esteemed prize of being whole again, providence was a blind spot, upon which I've been standing.

I was separated. From mum's presence, my dog, my room, our folk, our houses, gardens and bougainvillea, all dried up over years... It's hard to be a witness from a far distance, bearing all things you grew up with fading without your presence. It's not hard to imagine, let me be honest, the only reason you don't understand, is that you don't care.

The question trails me to this day, to this park; if I knew I could not return, would I have turned right around and stayed then? If I could speak my mind, freely then sure why not. But what can one unlearn?

Some back home will always blame you for leaving and you're not exactly very welcome or accepted where you immigrated. See, they would prefer you shushed as they tell your story. Yet I learned that any spectre of colour is made by its opposites, and abstracted alone.

I was a mess at weddings, I missed many funerals. I sat out drunk and dusted on pavements, like a beggar, empty palms reaching for love so far out yet so short within. I was shamed, uprooted, untamed. A reluctance to let go, delayed dreams to be remade.

No matter where I moved, melancholy remained put. Right back home where I battled not to forget, so I kept it close. I feared so the feeling of loss that it kept finding me all along, till I was stripped naked, till I was forlorn from hopes that it could all one day be reborn; like a baby new born, wailing, I wept, as everything slipped and sunk like the twilight zone to the bone.

IV

That's how I retreated to this wild island, this here park,
where privacy was respected and you could be who you
wanted to be; only if you had the guts to stand by what you
are not. I worked on, for the most part as an activist, trying
to push back somehow. I lived in bohemian monasteries,
behind red brick walls in rooms crammed ever smaller in
ramshackle, old factory turned communes. Losing weight by
the pound from eating too little and a continuous lack of clean
cutlery, we absolved escapism ceremonially and loosened
our drive as the money crept in all around. We attempted to
escape from our dues, monetary, moral, spiritual, historical or
other, hiding from that towering clock.
Personas held up in the commune, on the island, in the park
but dissolved outside it. This kept people coming back.

I retreated to this island, where I was not always welcomed
but accepted. To this city, where aggression in the form of
ruthless ambition ruled, class system stood, firm, where
the best in their trade flocked to become the best at what
they do and all hell broke loose on the lowly and the meek,
where a feudal underbelly was sugar-coated by an excess
of smiles and a flashy modesty; with sincerity largely left to
be found across countless pubs dotted around the streets for
all those in a hurry to and from the sun. I grew to love this
island, nonetheless, for and through all those who imagined
it something beautifully else, as its rains tapped and wiped
down rose coloured lenses and gifted us each a piece of its
sweet bitterness.

V

Living is an ebb and tide,
between a sense of meaning in anything or nothing at all.
The way I see it now,
having had something once, you can't lose it entirely.

I had a dream last night,
we were sailing on a boat with mum and dad,
the sun was up and all shining sharp across the sky,
we were riding high, the sails filled firm.
I was frightened for I hadn't learnt yet
to pull the ropes and how they kept us afloat,
mum and dad hanging on until their hands bled.

Cutting through a tamed sea eventually
we anchored ashore, and got in our beat-up car,
our dog Tarçın, long deceased, jumped in and we journeyed,
listening to 'Love Me Do' again.
When we reached the destination, I asked how we would get in
and mum said the borders were all deserted.
So we drove all the way to our old summer home,
the fresh forest and the hills rising luscious, the loud cicadas.
It was the first warm day of summer, and everyone could feel it,
it was where I learned to love,
we were happy like we had forgotten how to be.

We were childlike,
laughing as we started to fill the empty pool up,
which in truth was long sealed up.
Slowly the crystal waters rose and could overflow
and we dipped back into its clear womb to rest,
free at last.

My purest joy is buried in the abyss
but it springs a life, now, for better or worse,
"like the earth through the bodies of worms"
like the clocktower, through the bodies, that are ours
to harness.

RINCON DE LA VICTORIA

Corner of victory where the reconquering of Spain ended.
Like my own wars, where the East and West within,
clashed constantly,
like the waves between Morocco and Spain.

The loss was not men gallantly dying,
or women quietly paying costs of war,
but a slow yielding, to the overriding fate of geography.
Liberty never attained but searched for ceaselessly,
at the cost of many,
as bitterness, like rotten food, settles in our taste;
the cruel state of our world today, we digest every day,
as we remember the times when
"the vitality of the shell concealed the rot within".[8]

Rincon de la Victoria, a truce from wars sure to resume again.
Until then, this shoreline is meant for the mend,
from what's been spent: a salvation by beauty.
Eventually just to be,
feels hard earned when it shouldn't have been.
It was obscene.
But there are corners where victory prevails,
if you're not in it to win anything,
where one is enabled, if for a while
to live in a long-held dream.

8 The quote is from a poem by Jorge Olivera, a Cuban poet prosecuted for his writing and campaigned for by PEN International. He has kindly granted permission for this quote to be used.

WHAT IS HOME?

Home is a coagulation, so the answer to the question,
in a sense, eludes when asked.
There are many answers but after all,
home is remembering yourself.

Is home happiness, I wonder, then are we forsaken when sad?
Or if it is love, when it gushes like a waterfall,
what of its dry seasons?
If it's on the road, can it be moulded from dust and dirt,
wheels and rails, unlearnt at every new destination?
If it's between four walls, will it not age into a cage?
If it's a carnival will its music not become deafening?
And if it is the moment, here and now,
will it not slip through our empty palms
and clenched fingertips like sand?

Ever more it seems, home is remembrance.
The entirety of the long journey behind me.
Stronger the scent, more vivid the sensation
the further I look back,
my mother's warmth, my childhood home,
those places which formed
the shelter of self within.

Home, can it be the last or the first place I've been?
But more likely, it's somewhere in-between,
in remembrance, I say
like a puzzle, with
each piece entrapped by its meaning to the rest.

Home is what remains through the days of Wonder,
to those of boredom.

It's refuge from retreat.
A reeling from being bewitched
by what's next,
an unravelling from the siege
of your exaggerated reach,
it's being contempt.

Home is the body,
especially when the mind drifts astray,
cloaked in what has been,
peeled by what's to come.

Home is a closed door, behind which you can keep score.
Home is acceptance, by others first and last by yourself.

Home is not understood without leaving it
or losing it too.

Home is remembering an abyss
of lingering happenings,
like your fingertips, hands and legs
that carried you to these days,
still reaching, miles down the darkness –
It is memories,
like that of childhood swings,
keeping the same thrill whenever you find them again.

Home is the blue,
the earth's asylum from a cosmic vacuum.
Home is a cradle, that I no longer fit,
but keeps me restless still –
It radiates brighter the further I get from it.
Home is life before death,
and is at best a guess, until we pass.

THE LIGHTHOUSE

The lighthouse facing the distance,
punctures a wayward storm,
thrusting a jagged flash through its murky heart,
like a piercing arrow, sky bleeding rain.

The distant beam shepherd's dreams
of fine worked wooden ships sailing
violently downstream.
I hear the sailors pulling tight on cutting ropes
at rocking boats larger than their lives.
Between the mouths of wrathful waves
and the chiselled cliffs of home,
I stand on the shore, naked from the alarm,
if for a moment,
waving a white handkerchief – a belated farewell
and start to see by moonlight.

In the tavern, over the blaze in a stone-lined hearth,
under dulled chandeliers,
the travellers clumsily chase their best guess
at who anyone is.
While the riptides out at sea
sound deep from the belly of the beast
as people fight to claim the soul of the age
in the bottom of cups.

I stare blank,
thinking at the eyes of the lighthouse, set afar at sea,
shepherding wayward armadas on perilous pilgrimages.
No one blinks an eye when one ship is lashed
and capsized,
its woodwork crackling like broken teeth.

Music starts, a medieval tone,
like a proud daughter, the musician takes the lead
singing as though she was walking through the rye,
a blunt, rusted sickle, her tender voice,
reaping her harvest.
My pupils undulate to her moves
in echoes of melodies, spilled like a vast ocean,
her audience sways left and right,
to her ebb and tide.
Our truths hung alongside the coats out back.

That's my dream, she sings on
to find the fire in my mind.
Though with our feelings
we retreat each evening into drink,
not that we can forget the pain,
and the sun rides chivalrous
each morning, not that much can ever remain.

After the show, we meet and prolong a handshake
under the sanguine moon.
The moonlight chases her warm breath,
story lines slip and slide
as we stand on the edge of two lives
and two cigarettes burning out slowly,
eventually...
and a smile lingers,
like silken sunlight streaming over calmed sails,
on an ocean tamed,
after the storm.

I know well, how a lighthouse soaks up the darkness,
and a tavern lets it in,
and how so dearly she resembled someone, who loved
before the morning swallowed everyone,

like sailors at sea down below,
leaving only a life to keep,
handwritten in dried ink.

SOMETIMES I IMAGINE US ALL AS BABIES

Cradled side by side asleep, and I want to weep.
Like I did when my first dog died too early,
and I couldn't be with him. I hear his sickly wailing
when watching people
ripping each other's lives out, daily.
From boots breaking ribs for dominance,
to hearts charred from lust,
countless lovers have been broken to bits,
too long for any of us to remember it,
how were all once babies in our cradles,
side by side asleep.

In our life now,
where every aspect of vampire culture thrives,
desires ride high as needs get dry.
Some are jolted awake, by this crackling under;
through vicious storms, bombs or economic strife.
While others nonchalant, party on
the heights of earthly pleasures,
falling ever so deeply asleep in routine
until some tragedy cuts deep
and sets held back screams free.

I don't remember what turned you against me.
Thinking how you once seemed,
the kind-faced stranger smiling.
We don't let a glance slip anymore, let alone say
"hello, how are we?"
We were once cradled side by side asleep,
and now we're ashamed to address this growing suffering.
We try and spare the guilt, keep the innocence,
long as we keep from looking at the state of things.

As I try to do now imagining
once we were babies, cradled,
side by side asleep.

I want to weep tears of joy, new found love and regret,
for whatever we failed, we may yet succeed!
Learning of beauty, its sharp edges,
how it is lived, not attained.

But antidepressants keep me from the tears,
I'm overdue for such things.

I walk away from it all, the carnage and the parade,
lovingly,
for I knew why I was sent, long before reason cemented
I had to cherish happiness and find resolve,
seek help when I couldn't stand tall
and care for all as one and one for all,
from an insect to a lost soul.

All must have had love in them, once if not still I was sure,
but I was coy, in a bubble of my own.
I saw just how much misery was self-inflicted
by our dying breed, labelled "the nature of our being"
in the pursuit of transient victories.
But still sometimes
I envision us all as babies still, and I want to weep,
for the planet that we won't get to keep.

But I insist on this sight of us still side by side asleep,
because my hope holds, that underneath all differences,
seemingly cutting deep,
our similarities won't retreat but rise over the surface
the more we try to keep them buried.

Fear is hard to relieve, as we collectively take part in it.
It seems too much to bear, a better self, too late for more love to keep,
"a sense of compassion is a sign of being weak"
but I can see right through your tough masks,
scars and shiny cars Mr. and Mrs. "the world is mine"
who figure disaster is destiny's only master, I'll remind you that once
we were all babies, cradled side by side asleep
and it was a beautiful thing.

I'm privileged after all, that I still see beauty and cry after its tainting.
I see my mother crying instead of her only son,
now her mother and father are her babies.
Waiting for her with trembling hands, wetting pants,
confusing names and places.
Then I realize that soon, we will all be babies, again,
cradled side by side asleep.

And I want to weep, for the bitterness of running against time,
for nothing ever seems enough,
since someone started putting up fences around –

I imagine us all as babies, still in our cradles asleep,
with a sense of peace that we struggle to keep
yearning to be released and resonated with.

FOR MY BROTHER NEDIM

Written to poet and journalist Nedim Türfent on 29 November 2022, the day of his release from prison

Today, my brother Nedim Türfent is free after two thousand, three hundred and ninety-two days behind bars. Each day must have been sheer tyranny for him, especially when he was kept in solitary confinement.
He was my age now when they took him, 27. I try to imagine what I would do if I were imprisoned for the next six and a half years. I'm unable to fathom how I'd hold on as he did, to a light, to truth, to poetry, hope and solidarity, while much else decays and turns grim in the slow passing time of solitary confinement. Nedim, my brother, lived through all of this earnestly, innocently, as trial after trial relied on 18 secret witnesses to convict him, 17 of whom later testified their testimony was taken under torture.
Nedim wrote poetry, he wrote countless letters to me and many people across the country and the world, who wrote to him for support. He wrote back to each, tirelessly, month after month. Nedim wrote on, poetry, journalistic dispatches from jail, speeches to awards accepted abroad in his name. He wrote, as I moved cities, had love affairs and heart breaks, holidays, concerts, club nights, home cooked meals in friends' houses, walks in parks and by lakes, dinners and lunches out at favourite restaurants – it makes my blood boil, that all that and more was taken from him, simply because of his reporting.
I cannot fathom just how all this time, six and a half years, my brother Nedim has been behind bars, serving his young years as punishment, as a "traitor" for reporting on a military operation in the village of Yüksekova, running out of his house to document armoured vehicles pulling up in the dead of night. There Nedim saw, in search of a

fugitive, soldiers laying all the residents down handcuffed from the back onto the floor, stepping over them in black boots as the commander shouted: "You will see the might of the Turk!"

I bet all those villagers as much as Nedim and the rest of the world saw, through his camera, journalism, poetry and resilience, not exactly the might of the Turk but the tyranny unleashed in his name. There were 28 journalists in prison when Nedim was arrested, a year later the number jumped up to over 160 as Turkey become the biggest prison for journalists in the world. More than Egypt, China and Iran combined at the time. Part of the demonstration I assume, of the kind of might the commander was talking about.

The title of Nedim's first poem that I read was, 'Let my heart give life to the lifeless', he wished for his heart to have a "cold shower effect to the mummified ghosts roaming the country". This young man held unjustly, under horrendous conditions for years on end was consoling the reader in his poems. Comforting me in his letters for my troubles. This I still find astounding, like one of those moments 'When The Human Stars Shine' that Stefan Zweig wrote about. Of which there are countless, "miniscule cracks, through a titanic darkness."

I suggest strongly, dear reader, to read his poetry, honour his bravery and write to others unjustly imprisoned just like him. It doesn't need to be political, this activism, on the contrary, it can be very human. Remember well and don't go forgetting, the uphill struggle of truth, poetry and innocence against even the darkest forces, in the darkest places.

Take heed of Nedim Türfent, Lui Xiabo, Perhat Tursun and others like them. Their stance against all the odds. Although I never met him, I feel I know Nedim deeply through his kind, enlightened words he wrote, in his letters and his poetry. And I cannot wait to reunite with him in freedom as we dreamed for years since 2016 but regardless of course, he is already a brother to me as to many.

THE BACK SEAT OF THE CAR

When I was little, I always used to sit on the back seat of
our small red car. I would jump and shout to unfasten my
belt trying to see the front side. Yet I was also frightened
by the front seat because sometimes, my mum would
freeze at the questions I asked and sit there staring straight
ahead. After a while had passed, she would say things like
"I'm sorry?" I never understood why. I always wondered
what happened out there but failed to grasp it.

Years passed and I grew up. I went through the longing
for that front seat within me and that day finally came. I
remember pulling on the front door like a kid unravelling
his birthday present. I slowly leaned in and gently sat
down on the seat that seemed to be a dream. Now I could
see everything.

I didn't need to jump and shout to speak, the road was
clear as ice ahead of me yet I felt scared. I got lonesome,
suddenly there were fewer seats beside me. I was insecure.
The seatbelt that I once grappled to be saved from now
became a tightrope I hung on to. I got nervous. It was so
beautiful to imagine what lay ahead, that seeing it was
mostly traffic and barren land of concrete upset me.

As I looked out of that grand front window, I realized I had
no other seats left to dream of. That was it, more focus,
more responsibility, less time for questions.

Perhaps some things are better not to see. And truths are
bitter. Now I understand why my mother wouldn't listen
to me. She was so busy finding the right path that much
else seemed senseless in contrast. Now I also stared dead

straight down the path ahead and saw little else. To choose
the right one was as hard as accepting there being one at
all.

Now when I look at the back seat, I only feel a longing.
I remember being unable to see, the great liberty of
uncomprehending and the seats beside me. And you know
what? I miss the back seat a lot.

PERMISSIONS

Permission has been granted by my parents for their photograph to be used in this collection.

Thank you to Zehra Doğan for gifting me such a magnificent painting and allowing the image to be published here.

Many thanks to English PEN for allowing me to use a shortened version of my original article published with them, 'Home, Tarçın and my mother' published in *PEN Transmissions*, March 2019, English PEN's online magazine for international and translated literature.

Thanks to James Dowsett for the sharing of the poem 'Provides:' which we wrote together.

Many thanks to Cuban poet Jorge Olivera for the quote from his poem in my poem, 'Rincon de la Victoria'.

Other magazines publishing poems from this collection are: *Dutch DwB* in translation, 'What is Home' and 'Heading Down South'; and UK based *Bosla Arts*, 'High Art' and 'Brother Nedim'.

The poem, 'Li Du Man (What is Left Behind?)' was included in the online collaborative magazine *Li Du Man* which I designed and produced.

ACKNOWLEDGEMENTS

Thanks to the Black Spring Press Group and the sharpest editors one can ask for, Catherine Myddleton-Evans, and Todd Swift, for their work with me in giving a young writer the opportunity to debut.

Thanks to everyone who has encouraged and supported me throughout my life in various pursuits, there are too many to mention here but you know who you are.

And last but not least, thanks to you dear reader, for keeping this book alive.